JUV/E
TA
634
.S556
2003

HEGEWI

W9-BKV-715
Let's try it out with towers and bridges

DISCARD

Let's Try It Out

with Towers and Bridges

Hands-On Early-Learning Science Activities

by **Seymour Simon** and **Nicole Fauteux**

illustrated by **Doug Cushman**

Simon & Schuster Books for Young Readers
New York London Toronto Sydney Singapore

Note to Parents, Teachers, and Child-Care Providers

Let's Try It Out with Towers and Bridges introduces children to some basic construction techniques and shows them how to create model buildings that are strong and safe for the imaginary people who inhabit them. Through a series of experiments and other activities derived from play, children will acquire a basic understanding of the following concepts:

- *Solid construction makes for strong buildings.*
- *Strong foundations allow for lighter-weight construction and interior space.*
- *The strength of a bridge must increase with the distance spanned.*
- *Bending and folding increase the strength of a sheet of paper.*

The activities described in this book use these readily available materials:
- *wooden building blocks or other solid stackable objects*
- *modeling clay or dough*
- *plastic drinking straws*
- *sheets of paper (Use only one kind of paper so you can accurately compare the difference in strength created when the paper's shape is changed.)*
- *a ribbon or a jump rope*
- *a piece of corrugated cardboard*
- *tape*
- *paper clips or small plastic figures*
- *cotton balls or dry cereal*

Feel free to make substitutions and encourage the children to try the activities using other materials that come to mind. Build a large pyramid-shaped building from unopened tissue boxes instead of wooden blocks or create a tower by plunging tall candles into a layer cake.

SIMON & SCHUSTER BOOKS FOR YOUNG READERS
An imprint of Simon & Schuster Children's Publishing Division
1230 Avenue of the Americas, New York, New York 10020
Text copyright © 2003 by Seymour Simon and Nicole Fauteux
Illustrations copyright © 2003 by Doug Cushman
All rights reserved, including the right of reproduction in whole or in part in any form.
SIMON & SCHUSTER BOOKS FOR YOUNG READERS is a trademark of Simon & Schuster.
Book design by Greg Stadnyk
The text for this book is set in 19-point New Baskerville.
The illustrations are rendered in pen and ink, watercolors and gouache.
Manufactured in China
2 4 6 8 10 9 7 5 3 1
Library of Congress Cataloging-in-Publication Data
Simon, Seymour.
Let's try it out with towers and bridges / by Seymour Simon and Nicole Fauteux.
p. cm.
ISBN 0-689-82923-X
1. Structural engineering—Juvenile literature. 2. Bridges—Design and construction—Juvenile literature.
[1. Towers—Design and construction. 2. Bridges—Design and construction. 3. Structural engineering. 4. Models and modelmaking.]
I. Fauteux, Nicole. II. Title.
TA634 .S556 2003
624.1—dc21   2001020802

CHICAGO PUBLIC LIBRARY
HEGEWISCH BRANCH
3048 E. 130TH ST.   606

R0401857420

To my grandson Jeremy—S. S.

To my parents, Jacques and Bette Fauteux,
who instilled in me a love of good design
Thanks to Jason Liddell and the Panda Bears at
George Mason University's Child Development Center
for trying out these activities
—N. F.

To Libby and Spencer—D. C.

Imagine you are a pioneer heading west along a mountain ridge. There is not room for everyone to lie down in the wagon. So every evening you gather fallen branches and build yourself a shelter to sleep under.

Then one night a storm strikes. Rain trickles in between the branches. The wind begins to roar. You run to the safety of the wagon and crouch inside until morning.

When the sky finally clears, your house of sticks lies scattered on the ground. But nearby, trees still stand. The mountain has not moved.

A pioneer family might only need a shelter to last for one night.
But most families want houses that are built to last much longer.
Can you make model buildings that are strong like a mountain or a tree?
Let's try it out.

See if you can make a building in the shape of a mountain. Arrange wooden or large cardboard blocks to make a broad, solid base. Then add smaller and smaller layers of blocks. How strong is your building? Can it survive a windstorm?

Let's try it out.

Pretend you are the wind. Blow gently on your building, then harder. If each block is well supported, your building won't budge.

Over four thousand years ago, people built a group of giant buildings this way out of smaller and smaller layers of stone. They are called the pyramids and they are still standing today!

Can you imagine how it feels to be a block on the top of the building you made? **Let's try it out.**

Ask two friends to kneel on the floor right next to each other. Ask them to put their heads down and cover them with their hands. Now place your hands on their upper backs and gently climb on top of them.

Do you feel well supported up on the top? If your friends are close together and curled up tight, they will make a strong, steady base to hold you up.

Now switch places with one of your friends. How does it feel to be a block on the bottom? Do you feel the weight of the person on top? Now you know how strong the stones at the base of a building must be to support all the stones above.

Imagine you are a tall tree with many branches. Put your feet together and hold your legs straight like a tree trunk. Now reach up and out with your arms and let them sway like tree branches in the wind. Is it hard to keep your balance?

Trees don't balance on their narrow trunks. They have a strong base of roots hidden under the ground.

Find a plastic drinking straw or a cardboard tube and pretend it is a tree trunk. See if you can stand it on end. Will your pretend tree survive a strong wind?

Let's try it out.

Take a deep breath and blow on the straw or tube. Even a light breeze will probably knock it over.

See what happens if you push the bottom of your straw or tube into a lump of modeling clay or dough. Now your pretend tree is properly "rooted." It should survive even the biggest wind. Take a deep breath and try to blow it down!

Towers and other tall buildings have a strong base hidden under the ground. It is called a foundation.

Can you make a sturdy foundation for a skyscraper built from straws?

Let's try it out.

Make your foundation from a solid lump of modeling clay or dough. Then "root" your straws in the clay so they stand up straight and tall.

To finish your building, cut a few straws into shorter lengths. Then attach them to your upright straws with tape or little balls of clay.

Now try the strong wind test on your skyscraper. If it falls over, try strengthening your foundation with more clay. If you built a strong foundation, your building should stand like a well-rooted tree.

What happens when a tree falls across a stream? Animals can use it to get from one side to the other. But people need bridges to get across water. Can you build a bridge across a stream?

Let's try it out.

Find a piece of ribbon or a jump rope. Lay it down straight in front of you and place two large blocks on either side of your pretend stream. Now lay a piece of paper across the blocks.

If the bridge falls down, try pushing the blocks closer together. If the bridge stays up, try pulling the blocks apart so the paper can span, or reach across, a wider stream. Is it easier to build a bridge that spans a short distance or a long distance?

When you find a good length for your bridge, see if some pretend people can get across. You can use paper clips or tiny plastic figures. How many of them can your bridge hold before it falls down?

What do you think will happen if you change the shape of the paper? Will it make your bridge stronger?

Let's try it out.

Take a sheet of paper and arch or bend it between the two blocks. Does your arched bridge hold more pretend people than your flat paper bridge did? Use your pretend people to find out.

Arches are strong shapes. They make good bridges. But suppose you want a bridge that's flat.

Try folding the side edges of the paper. Do the folds make the bridge stronger?

What happens if you add more folds? Bend the paper back and forth to form pleats. Is your new bridge strong enough to cross a wide river? Pull the supporting blocks apart to find out.

A pleated bridge may be strong enough to support a toy car.

Lay a flat piece of paper over the pleated piece to make a smooth roadway. Then gently slide a toy car across your paper bridge.

Try driving a toy car across your other paper bridges. Which bridge is strongest? If all your bridges are the same length, the bridge with the most folds should hold the most weight.

Look at the edge of a piece of corrugated cardboard. In between the smooth outer layers is a piece of pleated paper. The many tiny bends in the paper make this kind of cardboard very strong like your pleated bridge.

Can you use what you learned about building bridges and towers to build a castle fit for a king and queen?

Let's try it out.

Take your blocks and get to work. Your castle must have strong walls to keep out enemies, but it cannot be solid. People need to be able to move around inside.

Your castle also needs a roof. Try using what you learned about building paper bridges to make a paper roof.

Lay pieces of paper across the tops of your walls. They can be flat, arched, folded, or pleated. What kind of roof do you think works best?

Your roof must be able to reach from one wall to the others, just like your bridge reached across the stream. If you cannot make your roof stay up, move your walls closer together or add new walls inside your castle. You will know the walls are the right distance apart when your roof rests comfortably on top.

Will your paper roof protect the king and queen in a snowstorm?

Sprinkle some pretend snow, like cotton balls or dry cereal, on top of your castle. How much weight can your roof support? If it collapses right away, try strengthening your roof by adding folds to the paper or arching it. No king or queen wants a castle filled with snow!

Builders need to make sure that houses don't fall on the people inside. Castle builders counted on thick stone walls to hold up the roof. Today builders use posts and columns to make buildings safe and strong.

Strong wooden posts in houses and upright steel columns in skyscrapers hold up the upper floors and the roof. You can't see these in most buildings, because they are hidden in the walls.

Can you use drinking-straw posts to make a strong house of paper?

Let's try it out.

Plant some straws in modeling clay or dough. Place some straws close together and others farther apart. Make walls by taping or clipping sheets of flat or folded paper to the straws. Finally place your favorite roof on top. See how many different kinds of houses you and your friends can build.

When your houses are built, blow on them. When strong winds blow, which house stands best? Does it matter how big your foundation is? Or how many straws you used? Does where you placed them make a difference? Does the kind of roof you used make a difference?

Yes! A builder needs to think about all these things when constructing a place for people to live.

Now that you know how to build with paper, blocks, and straws, you and your friends can build a small city with strong houses, towers, and bridges. Then have fun letting the "weather" do its worst!

Let's Try It Out with Towers and Bridges is structured so that teachers can present all the activities in a single session. With younger children, teachers may prefer to cover the material in several shorter sessions over the course of a week. Ideally, the class should be divided into small groups so that each child can fully experience the activities for himself or herself.

Parents and caregivers may find it more rewarding to use the book in shorter time intervals, pulling it off the shelf to introduce an activity when their children are already busy with blocks or modeling dough. The book can also stimulate ideas on how to create a house for a new stuffed animal or a garage for a favorite toy car.

The Let's Try It Out series integrates the scientific method into everyday life by using only safe, readily available materials and by modeling the experiments it presents on play. The books encourage children to use their body and their senses to explore their surroundings.

Parents and teachers can use these books to help children make observations in the course of their play, recognize the significance of these observations, and organize them in such a way that children can draw some preliminary conclusions about how things work in the fascinating world around them.

Parents and teachers should not be disturbed if children sometimes draw the wrong conclusions from these activities. Children's cognitive development varies greatly at young ages, and some children may not yet be able to grasp every concept presented. Forcing children to accept your explanation of a phenomenon they cannot understand will undermine your main goals of teaching them to observe carefully, form hypotheses, and test them. Chances are that if you reintroduce a challenging activity six months later, a child will be ready to draw the right conclusion for himself or herself.

You can also use the Internet to find out more about this book and others in the series. Visit our Web site at www.SimonSaysKids.com. We value your suggestions and comments about your experiences using our books with your children.

Seymour Simon
Nicole Fauteux